Th[illegible]'s
Tricks [illegible] Trade

Dog training manual

Thomas Golby BSc (Hons)

MAPLE PUBLISHERS

The Dog's Tricks of the Trade

Author: Thomas Golby

First Published in 2024

ISBN 978-1-83538-159-5 (Paperback)
978-1-83538-160-1 (Hardback)
978-1-83538-161-8 (E-Book)

Book cover design, Illustrations and Book layout by:
White Magic Studios
www.whitemagicstudios.co.uk

Proofreader: Julie Badger

Published by:
Maple Publishers
Fairbourne Drive, Atterbury,
Milton Keynes,
MK10 9RG, UK
www.maplepublishers.com

A CIP catalogue record for this title is available from the British Library.

Professional Disclaimer

The purpose of this book/manual content is to inform and entertain. The content cannot and does not contain dog welfare recommendations. Any dog welfare content is for general information and education purposes only. Subsequently, before taking any actions based on our content, we encourage you to contact a vet or the appropriate licensed professional. If you are uncertain about your or your dog's ability to safely perform any of the techniques or tasks described in this book, you should first consult and medical or veterinary professional

UNDER NO CIRCUMSTANCE SHALL WE HAVE ANY LIABILITY TO YOU FOR ANY LOSS OR DAMAGE OF ANY KIND INCURRED AS A RESULT OF THE USE OF THE CONTENT OR RELIANCE ON ANY INFORMATION PROVIDED IN THIS BOOK. YOUR USE OF THE INFORMATION PROVIDED AND YOUR RELIANCE ON ANY INFORMATION IN THE BOOK/ MANUAL IS SOLELY AT YOUR OWN RISK. THOMAS GOLBY (THE AUTHOR OF THIS BOOK) DOES NOT AND CANNOT ASSUME ANY RESPONSIBILITY FOR INJURY OR DAMAGE TO PROPERTY DUE THE MISUSE OR MISINTERPERTATION OF THE INFORMATION PROVIDED IN THIS BOOK.

TABLE OF CONTENTS

Introduction

This book is aimed to share the tricks used by dog trainers and to give you an understanding of how training your dog can be fun and rewarding.

Whilst reading and hopefully learning from this manual please remember, there is **never only one method** to train a dog. Therefore, I encourage you to take the knowledge you have learnt from this book and develop on it. You can share it with others so they may learn what you have found. When it comes to dog training the truth is there is **always something new to learn**. Even the most experienced dog trainer can learn something new about dog training. I can guarantee if you put the effort into training your dog you will build a stronger relationship and a better understanding of your dog.

Training with your dog can lead to many opportunities and allows you to improve upon the training methodology learnt. You can get creative and develop new training techniques that will most likely impress other dog trainers like myself. So, go out there and train and bond with your dogs.

Before going any further into this dog training manual, it is important to understand the reason for writing this book. This book is a manual on basic dog training, the assumption is you have some idea on dog behaviour and body language. There will be a bit of information provided on dog behaviour, but we are not going to discuss this in-depth. Whilst understanding your dog's behaviour is an important topic, it would be ineffective to only write it down. Dogs are individuals and will require face to face demonstration

to explain and comprehend their individual behaviour. This topic is not cut and dry so, we have chosen not to discuss this in the manual, but instead recommend consulting a local professional.

After reading this dog training manual it is hoped that you, the reader, take away a few things. One of which is that dogs truly are amazing creatures that could help us humans even more than we could possibly or currently know. However, do not be mistaken, it takes time to teach them and it can be hard for some to teach a dog. The dog we see on social media or on TV have had trainers/owners who have put in a lot of time to get them like that and each one of those people will be keeping a secret from us all, which is the indescribable bond that they have developed through time and training. So, give it a go, you and your dog can go far and achieve amazing goals whatever age they are.

It is also important to know what resources are at your disposal which will assist in your dog's training and mental wellbeing. This is a topic that the manual will explain in more depth. An example of this is dog day care companies. A facility that will become a pinnacle location for the local dog communities and the opportunities they provide to dog owners and dog trainers.

This book will also reveal the insight of a dog trainers world and most importantly will explain what to expect from future services. Dog day care is becoming a fundamental facility for dogs and online dog community platforms. They are a local supportive establishment that brings the local dog community together resulting in reduction of undesirable behaviours, especially in negative social interactions. They are businesses that have transformed in a single decade to become part of every dog owner's welfare care plan. Owners and trainers will need to use these resources as part of their training solutions.

Building a strong functional relationship with the dog in question is a key goal. This is not a fast-track solution to all your dog problems, as learning the fundamentals are imperative. In fact, symptoms like dog aggression can be solved by going back to basic training, just like if were giving a problematic computer a reboot. Therefore, it is important to seek help with a person who has the experience and muscle memory to communicate naturally with your dog. Take on board what is being written in this manual, but if you feel out of your depth, do not be ashamed, please contact a dog trainer. If ignored or done incorrectly, complex behaviours like dog aggression can escalate.

Truths about dog training

Welcome to The Dog's Tricks of the Trade, we are here to help dogs and their trainers. Before we begin, please remember a few things whilst going through each section of this training manual. Dogs are individuals like us, and all learn at their own rate. Spending time training our dogs will create a bond. The bond between dog and human can become strong if worked upon. One of the aims of this manual is to illustrate strategies and the tools to have an amazing relationship with your dog and allow you to really get to know their personality. So, as we begin it might be worth mentioning early on that dogs in general like to see your eyes, therefore it is better to start off without wearing sunglasses. Also, never hide your hands with your sleeves as it can make unfamiliar dogs nervous around you. Trust me, it is always worth pulling your sleeves up quite literally, we want to make good first impressions when it comes to dogs.

You probably hear phrases in dog training such as leading, alpha or control whilst reading through various dog training manuals like this one, but it seems to me that this can be misinterpreted which leads to so many problems for dogs whilst they receive training from their owners. Even though we will get into this important topic in more depth later, it is important we clearly understand what dog trainers are getting at. It is all about the dog's perception and how they perceive the social structure around them which is what is most important. This means that the human idea of what makes a good leader/Alpha must be left and forgotten, as it bears no relevance to how a **dog thinks**.

A dog under the owner's control can only be defined as a dog that trusts and respects you. The dog shows this by **listening** to you and illustrates **good manners around you**. The idea that a dog will act the same for everyone is a myth and is simply not true. You must work with the dog to get results that is why it is essential to realise when you require a service from a local dog trainer. You must be committed to put the time into supporting the work the trainer has achieved with the individual dog. Dog trainers and their techniques will help you to form a connection with your dog. The truth is dog trainers will use methodology and experience to assist you and your dog in the right direction. But if you are not willing to continue their teachings after the training sessions then in all honesty you are wasting your money and the trainer's time.

So, let's investigate control a bit more and how this manual determines what this means. If you have control, **YOU SHOULD NEVER HAVE TO REPEAT YOURSELF.**

Which means if you find that you are constantly repeating yourself with a specific instruction, go back to the basics. If your answer is that you cannot be bothered then it's entirely your fault, do not blame the dog. As a dog owner you lead and control every situation. In truth the dog needs to be able to trust you enough to deal with any situation. Being able to master the basics is getting you on the road to obtaining the dog's trust which is why the following advice is so **important.** It doesn't matter how bad the situation is that you find yourself in, screaming and acting erratically will ruin the trust the dog has in you and will cause the dog to act out in undesirable ways. Controlling your own emotions helps the dog feel safe and calm. I know it is easier said than done however it is essential to keep your emotions in check for the dog's sake.

Also, just to confirm **age does not come into it**, so please don't think your old dogs cannot learn a new trick or behaviour.

Another worthy mention as we get further into the training aspect of this manual is not to give up with a chosen training method too quickly. The longer it takes for a dog to learn what you want her or him to do, the better the understanding of the task given. It is very easy to confuse a dog so if you change the methods too quickly and too often, it will make the dog's job a lot harder to understand what you want them to do or want from them. **Give the dog time**, they will get there.

Get the most out of your dog

1. Use his or her daily amount of dinner as a reward
2. Say a command once clearly, don't say it repeatedly
3. Make the command clear, don't say "sit down". Do you want the dog to sit or go down?
4. Be positive, energetic, and joyful when the dog achieves their goals

Rules about food

If you are keen on set meals in the day, then please abide by the following. This also applies to picky eaters. The food given to the dog should be provided with a command. Get the dog to wait for their dinner in a sit position. Whilst the dog is acting calm and respectful then put the bowl of food on the floor. At this point the dog must wait until you give the order to approach the food. **It is important to remember, food cannot stay there until the dog is hungry.** They get about 2 minutes to start eating and if they choose not to eat their food it gets taken away. This does mean that the dog will not be fed later, the dog needs to understand that food is given under your choice. If an owner wants a dog to behave with food, it must believe that is has worked for it in some form which means that you must be strict.

Just a personal note I do not recommend raw diets. That is my opinion, take it as you like it. That is unless you are talking about a controlled raw food diet produced by a company that has taken the full dietary requirements into account. If you are not sure, please ask your local veterinarian. In my opinion companies that make dry food have spent a lot of money to produce the perfect kibble, using the latest science and research. Therefore, I would personally use dry feed for dogs every time.

How a dog learns

Research has indicated that domestication of the dog was about 33,000 years ago which means the dogs we know today have adapted to understand us very well. They have an ability to read our body language, hand gestures, vocal commands and most importantly our emotions. All these traits get our attention and make them affectionate human companions. **Out of all the domestic species humans have created, the dog is the most diverse and useful.** Dogs are so well adapted to live and work with humans that they can even pick up on our emotions even when we think we are hiding them. So, when we are training our dogs, remember that if we get **frustrated, the dog will stop learning and focus on that.**

Why do they stop learning, you might ask? Because they want to please us as the dog trainer and now you are getting frustrated and annoyed. Would you be able to learn in that situation? I am not saying it is not easy to get frustrated. Just stop the training and take five minutes and start again.

Dogs are individuals and learn at their own pace. Take my personal dog that I have right now, she does not learn as quick as other dogs I have trained. So, it requires me to go slower and take my time with her. Like us all dogs are different. In most cases, the longer the time you take to teach the dog a command the better the dog will understand it in the long run, which means there is no need to rush. **Short and intense training sessions work better. Therefore, give you and the dog breaks regularly.**

Now, on the more serious parts of the dog's mind. When training a dog, we need to think about the dog's perception. There are rules that we need to live by which will hold value to our dogs. For example, **we never let a dog go through a doorway first,** dogs always must show respect to humans of all ages. Respect and politeness for a dog's social network are both important values that must be learnt and understood by the owner. Therefore, it is important to socialise our dog at a young age.

All undesirable behaviours have been taught in some description. Which means they will need to be untaught to treat what we perceive as an undesirable behaviour. A good example of this is allowing a puppy to jump up at you, then expecting the dog to know that now it is an adult, is has become too large for this behaviour. Even though this is an important factor to dog mentality and their thinking process it also has its safety advantages as well.

The secret guide

You are probably looking at the key secret guide and thinking what is this. If you follow this system correctly it is guaranteed you will see improvements with your four-legged best friend.

This secret guide only works when the order is followed one after the other. Therefore, using a local dog trainer is preferable for most people, as they will most likely use this methodology.

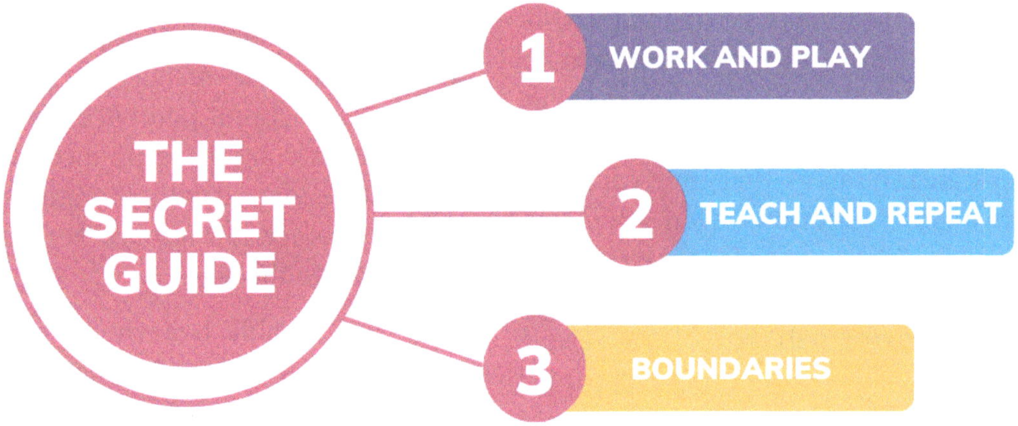

Work and Play

Exercising the body is the first step, this will let them burn off their energy of the day before any training begins. This can be done by running or playing with toys, for example throwing a ball or playing tug of war. The idea is that this part is fun and gets them into a routine. Dogs love routines so use this to your advantage.

Teach and Repeat

Now you should have a tired dog in front of you. They have played and should have used some of that energy. Before you start this part of the training program you need to have the dog in a calm and controlled mindset/ temperament. This is important because we want the dog to be listening. If you have got a dog that is still bouncing around calm yourself by taking deep breaths and ignoring the dog. This will transfer your calm energy to the dog whilst you hold the lead. After a few moments of remaining calm the dog will start to get the point and begin to show the behaviour you can work with. Again, remember it is all about fixing a routine. After a few times of the routine the dog will start finding the process easier.

As mentioned, excitement and energetic behaviour that is brought to the session needs to be controlled as we are here to learn something with our dogs. However, it is important that this is not misunderstood, the training session should be fun and enjoyable. If the dog has brought bouncy energy, we do not add to it. Once you feel the crazy energy has died down then slowly start the training process. We calmly reward the dog learning each step in a calm and controlled manner. Dogs will eventually develop a sort of working mode behaviour, but this takes time and patience. When you have reached this stage, push on the training techniques that require higher energy rewards.

Do not be afraid to repeat exercises, as this will assist the dog's confidence whilst performing each task asked of them. When they can perform a given task well, reward them as it makes the dog enjoy the training process. Another key part of the guide is to look out for tasks that the dog struggles with. These are areas you and your dog can focus on. However, it is always important to bear in mind any health issues that might prevent them from performing tasks. Going back to the training aspect please remember the follow saying **if it's not hard, it is not worth doing**. All dogs have a task they struggle to understand, but that is where we can discover how our dogs learn best and which methodology reveals the best results out of them. This is what makes a good dog trainer. A tailored training regime will benefit the dog and trainer.

Dogs learn in short intense bursts. Which needs to be applied whilst training your dog. This means that your dog will learn better with frequent breaks. This allows you to think ahead and evaluate the current situation whilst your dog gets a well-earned break.

Another important question you should ask yourself is, "Where should I do most of this training, should I choose a different location every time?" Let this manual answer that question for you. It would be advisable to choose a single location for all the attempted training whilst starting off, especially when performing the basic tasks. This will help put the dog into a working mind frame. This location needs to be chosen for tactical reasons as well. You need an area where you can control the environment as much as possible.

Finally, and most importantly, please remember this is meant to be fun. So, reward as much as possible. Don't be afraid to ignore or show disappointment if the dog is not performing correctly. Never tell them off during training, this is important because we want the dog to express themselves. If the dog is not focused go back the first step of the guide and drain some of their energy once again.

Boundaries

The first mistake that can be made is thinking this part of training means telling your dog off. It means the opposite; it means providing high reward energy for correct behaviour. Remember at this stage, the dog should be quite tired by now and has not really got the energy to question or push boundaries.

Training these boundaries are going to be easier, due the lack of energy. Now at this point your probably thinking what boundaries can I set? Obviously, every individual living environment will require different boundaries. However, here are some ideas that might be useful to you:

Do not cross the threshold is a good way to show boundaries that will become lifesaving. It is also a way to keep dogs behind doorways without closing the door. You might be asking yourself how would I go about doing this?

Firstly, we need to start off the lesson safely, therefore we won't be using the front door that most likely leads onto a road. At this point you have chosen a safe door that leads outside and now we can begin. Now it is time to maintain an invisible boundary that the dog must not cross. The idea is to keep the dog from crossing the doorway. During this exercise it is more powerful when the trainer does not give verbal commands and lets the dog slowly figure out what you are wanting. Now we begin by standing sideways to the dog and having the dog on the lead. The dog will often try to go past you but as soon as the dog goes past the doorframe, grab hold of the lead and **gently guide** the dog back over the doorway and repeat this process. You can block the dog's movements by stepping sideways in front of them occasionally. But again, it is more powerful if you say nothing. It can take time for the dog to recognize and stay behind the invisible line. Allow the dog time to think, they will get this exercise if you give them time. After the exercise has been completed, it then becomes your job to invite them over the line. Remember this doorway must become a black and white scenario where they must have your invitation to pass every time.

Another boundary that would be useful in theory is don't chase livestock. As you can imagine this training can be applied to anything such as the family cat, but the premise is all the same. In most cases the family cat has already illustrated to the dog it is not a great idea to mess with them. However, just in case your dog likes to chase pets or wildlife, the following information might come useful to you.

First step is to have the dog on a lead. The most important factor of learning this boundary is that no animal is harmed during this training process. We are training the dog not to chase things and we are going to do this by giving as little amount of instruction as possible. We don't want to be making too much sound or words just in case the dog mistakes it as encouragement. The trainer will be required to devote time and patience, whilst calmly proceeding with the ongoing instruction. The **dog on the lead** will be shown the cat in this example and rewarded when the dog stops trying to energetically interact with the cat. If the dog pulls on the lead or shows signs of a prey drive, use the lead to turn them away by walking in the other direction with encouragement. Repeat this by using your body and lead to control the dog's movements. The idea is we want to reward the dog when their attention is taken off the cat. If this is found difficult, contact a local dog trainer to give you the visual demonstration required for you to continue when you are on your own.

Here are some more suggestions:

1. Don't bark at neighbouring dogs or people.
2. Don't go into the kitchen when I am cooking
3. Stay on the dog bed until I have finished my dinner

All these suggestions should give you the ideas on what boundaries can be put in place. If you make the experience positive your physically and mentally tired dog will happily respond to your commands, which will build a mindset of obedience once it comes to day-to-day living. Please remember all good things take time.

In truth the only way this system has not worked is if you have not performed it correctly. It is never the dog's fault; they are just coming along for the ride. If the individual dog seems to be having a problem, please review yourself first and see what you're doing wrong.

Boundaries need to be considered in all household for dogs of all ages. Therefore, boundaries gets promoted by so many dog trainers. Remember boundaries do not have to be complex, it can be as simple as telling a dog when and where play can occur. An example of this is not allowing play in the lounge. This does have a valid reason behind it. It's set into the dog's mind how the environment around them works. This example will allow you to relax in your lounge or chat without a dog distracting you or causing a problem. Most importantly, this gives you the owner an extra tool which will allow you to control the dog in a situation that might require it.

Hearing the NO word

As a dog trainer I hear so many people say that a dog should not hear the word no. I personally do not believe in the theory. Dogs need to know when they have done something wrong and when they have done something right. A dog's social network has a strict social structure, which can be described as a network which requires all members to follow rules about being polite to each other and these rules must be met by all adult dogs. These might sound weird, and we are going to get into this in more depth later, but it is important to know dogs do tell each other off to prevent a situation from escalating into something damaging to an individual. In a nutshell stopping a fight before it can occur.

So, we have determined that dogs actively tell each other off for undesirable behaviour. Now it is important to know how we say NO to a dog. Lets say your dog is about to chew on an electric cable, I don't think I need to tell you how dangerous this can be. Therefore, you need to tell the dog off. The trick is the less you tell the dog off the more effective it will be when used. You see the dog chewing on a cable, as the owner or trainer you need to act immediately. It is important whilst instructing the dog that you always look and feel in control. The dog will respect your requests and instruction if you act in control. Please note, if you get aggressive or angry with the dog, they will not learn the important lesson. A "no" said loud enough that is not coming out as anger will be enough of a lesson. If the word is said with confidence, it will mean more to the dog than if it is repeated. Repeating the word "no" makes it mean nothing. Now you have told the dog off, the next step is to **calmly** take the dog away from the offending cable.

At this point the dog has dropped the cable and has gone with you. Which means the dog has done what you wanted it to do right? Therefore, praise him or her for going along with your instruction.

Dogs learn in the moment, telling a dog off after it has taken place just teaches the dog fear and, in some cases, overshadows the crime committed in the first place. The trick is to not let the telling off stay negative. It is worth thinking about the negative behaviour itself, in some instances the dog might be pushing boundaries. That is why it is important to have black and white rules, and never give in to the dog especially if the negative behaviours are aimed towards getting attention from you. Dogs will test people to see what they can get away with. Therefore, they might go back to the offending item more than once. In this case the "no" is applied again, never break. Never allow the dog to see your breaking point. **No means no** which might sound simple but is so true. Let's say you're dealing with a dog who gets pushy and starts acting as if the offending behaviour is a game. Which is causing you to feel overwhelmed and start losing your control. Therefore, it would be advisable to use isolation. Removing the dog to another room and isolating them breaks the dog in their stride and gives you the ability to recompose yourself. This is important when you find yourself struggling with maintaining the control. Always remember if you find yourself getting annoyed by the dog's behaviour take a 5-minute break. Once the isolation has occurred, use distraction so they move on to something else, unless you are wanting it to be a trainable moment. Dogs do not live in the past and telling them off for something in the past is pointless and unhelpful to your training therefore timing your discipline action is key to producing an effective outcome.

In conclusion, the dog needs to know the word no. However, it should hear good boy or good girl more often. But **in no instance does this book state that you should hit a dog**, especially as a form of punishment. Additionally, this manual does not need to go into the definition of hitting, it is quite self-explanatory. For your information negative physical reactions teaches negative physical reaction. If you have a Caucasian Shepard, Kangal, Boerboel or a Tibetan mastiff that is frankly a death sentence for who owns them as they respond like for like.

The difference between male and female dogs

There are many factors that affect a dog's thinking process including whether they are male or female. The differences are normally subtle however it is important to know the differences. Hopefully the following information will highlight these small behaviour differences and help to determine any necessary changes to the training strategy. The following descriptions of traits of males and females may not apply to every dog due to environmental variables and other factors.

Male

Dog: In specific breeds males are often larger in size.

Castrating: There are positive outcomes of castration, for example medically (which would be best discussed with your local vet) however regarding behaviour there is not up to date research that can confirm castration has direct links to changing a dog's behaviour such as their aggression levels. The only behaviour that will be affected is the hormone driven ones such as humping. From a dog trainer perspective, any type of aggressive behaviour will always need training intervention. In truth castration does not help a dog change behaviour. If we consider that if castration was the main solution to male dog aggression most uncastrated dogs would be unapproachable or would be prone to aggression. If you are thinking of castrating your male dog that is fine but please do not do it solely for behaviour reasons. Speak to a local dog trainer near you and seek out their assistance on the matter. **Any form of dog aggression is never a quick fix.** Please be aware that this manual would also suggest that behaviour issues should always be checked by a qualified veterinary individual to ensure that there are no medical links to the behaviour issue. **Vets and Vet Nurses are qualified professionals and are the only source that should be used for medical issues.** It would be suggested that solving dog behaviour issues by solely castrating a male dog is not the solution.

Work: Dependent on the breed, has a great work ethic.

Dominance: Space control. Males will tend to show dominance and control through claiming space around them.

Female

Bitch: Often smaller in most breeds compared to the male.

Spaying: This is where it becomes complicated. Now yes spaying will change her behaviour, however it is not as cut and dry as you think. Female dogs behave differently whilst they are in season and during this time, they will alter their behaviour and interactions with male dogs around them. This is regardless of whether a male is castrated or not, therefore spaying a female would eradicate these biological behaviour changes. Medically there are benefits to spaying a female and it is best to discuss these with your local vet. This includes preventing pyometra (infection of the uterus) and removing the risk of ovarian cancer.

Work: Dependent on the breed, has a great work ethic

Dominance: Through object control. This form of dominance is seen so differently by the different sexes. An omega female can take an object from an alpha male without it meaning anything to the alpha male.

The law on commands and boundaries

Commands and boundaries can never be broken. This is one of the most important rules in this manual. For example, if you do not want your dog to go up the stairs, the dog can never go up the stairs. The dog's world is black and white, either they can do it, or they can't do it. If you do allow your dogs to break this rule or break this rule by inviting them up the stairs, you become unpredictable to the dog. This makes them nervous which can then lead to other undesired traits occurring. If you don't believe this to be fact, please speak to a dog trainer. They will tell you the importance of maintaining the rules.

So, the idea that we are only going to be using positive reinforcement is wrong. Dogs need a firm and fair voice that will encourage them to be well behaved but be equally strong and firm when they misbehave. The firm tone of our voice can be a tool which is most effective when followed with an instruction.

Desirable traits and tricks

All behaviours are learnt in some way, it could be from mum, sibling, owner, other people, traumatic situations, or the environment. It is easy to see how undesirable behaviours are created.

Before you set off and perform some amazing training techniques like scent tracking, canicross or agility training, you will need to have a basic relationship with your dog. This means that your dog should be at a stage where the dog is hanging on to your every word, giving you that element of control and respect.

I have given you some tricks to master. All these tricks or skills will come in useful in other situations and will give you that bond we all desire with our dogs. These are the tricks to master:

1. Watch
2. Walking correctly
3. Sit
4. Down
5. Bed
6. Heel
7. Recall
8. Wearing a muzzle

These tricks can also be seen as a **foundation of basic training techniques** that allow the dog owner to progress onto more difficult tasks.

Now if you're saying to yourself, I have not got time for all of this. The only question that should be asked to you is why you bought this dog training manual.

Dog training takes time and effort. If you cannot give your dog these two essential gifts, then please do not expect the dog to perform at a high level. In truth these basic skills are the building blocks to all training and behaviour tasks. These foundations of training are where we stop your dog from pulling on the lead, barking at the TV or being aggressive to a person. You will find more information on these basic training techniques further on in the manual, but please first take in the following chapter.

Reward system

There are many ways we can reward our dogs during the training process. Using more than one method can make training with our dogs more effective.

It will be mentioned throughout this manual to provide the dogs with a high energy reward. This means you show excitement and happiness towards the dog when they have achieved something big. This is directed towards most dogs which do not have high reactive reactions to positive rewards. An illustration of a dog with a high reactive response would be a dog that constantly jumps up, has constant high energy exertion or is biting/nibbling through overwhelming stress. In conclusion a dog that struggles to control itself with excitement. If your dog is like this, then giving it a high energy reward would not be the best idea. In fact, it will most likely bring the dogs attention away from the exercise we are trying to teach them.

Our dogs require our attention, they should only be getting this when we want it to be given. Therefore, we can use this as teaching tool. Dogs love our attention so much and we like their attention, which means using it as a reward system can benefit our training.

There are a few other reward systems we can choose from. Toys and food treats are some examples we can use that create excitement leading to physical affection. Most of these options sound obvious but it is the way we use them that makes them effective tools.

It is advisable to use their daily dinner food as the treat throughout the day. This does mean that the dogs will not be receiving set time feeding. After maintaining these changes, you will notice your dog's mind set change into a working one. The idea that the dog will have to work for its food will motivate them to perform and bring excitement towards their training and play sessions.

Working in the UK as a dog trainer has provided the opportunity to meet some owners that do not believe that dogs should be worked on for food. However, it would be advisable to see it as resource as the dog is always going to be given the food anyway so it would make sense to use it as a tool. It results in the dog achieving simple goals whilst building a working mentality. Additionally, this feeding process will encourage a positive relationship with the dog. The mind frame of getting the dog to think it must work for its food provides a healthy balanced relationship that you are in control of. The dog knows you are the food provider when you give them set meals, but nothing else. Also, it is worth thinking about what caused domestication in the first place.

Humanity created the domesticated dog to perform useful roles with a working mindset and the breeds that met these requirements the best, survived and can be seen today. In the long run, if you do not want to use food as a treat system whilst following this helping guide, you are probably going to struggle a lot more. Be aware that over feeding can cause health problems, therefore it is your job as the owner to be responsible for measuring out their daily intake. Most food brands will give you a rough guide, so please use the instructions from the manufacturer.

Hand gestures

Hand gestures are important for dog training. It would be advisable to have a hand gesture for each command you want to teach your dog. For obvious reasons hand gestures for all training methods must remain constant when applying them to each command. This is especially important when using commands without words, for example the watch command which is one of the most fundamental training techniques to start with.

Watch

A dog watching an owner is an important skill. It is important because it lets us know as the human that we have the dog's attention. The watch command is one of the first we teach a dog. The purpose is so that we can direct the dog's attention every time we want to instil information and lessons into the dog's mind. A well-trained watch command can solve behaviour issues, such as a dog ignoring instructions whilst on walks.

It is important to know what we are expecting from the dog we are training. The aim of this task is for the dog to look at your eye when you ask them to. Showing the people that gave the command that they have their attention is a trait we want them to get used to for when we start doing more complex tasks like heel work.

The following step by step guide has been provided. Please take in the steps, actions, and tips as these are there to assist you.

STEP 1

Looking up at me

Firstly, choose a location where there are few distractions (controlled environment). We want the dog to understand that looking at your eye is a positive and rewarding behaviour.

Take a pinched treat between finger and thumb and bring the treat close to your face and say the command "watch". As soon as the dog looks up at the hand containing the treat give the reward.

Tips

- This task will require treats
- Clicker training can be useful in this task. If used correctly. Click just before the reward.
- Keeping the dog on a loose lead can help them in this situation.
- Making your voice positive and interactive will assist you in this step.
- This step requires quick reaction from you, when providing the reward.

STEP 2

Eye contact

Repeat the process but this time bring the treat in front of your eyes. After repetition, the dog should start to understand your intention. Try and keep the stare up to 5 seconds. Remember to take this slowly so please work it up to 5 seconds.

Tips

- Using a fun voice when giving the command will give you a better chance.
- Give you and the dog breaks.
- Keep the task fun.

STEP 3

Hand signals

Now use the hand signal. The best way to do this is to put a treat in the palm of the hand, whilst the index finger and middle finger point into your eyes. Now when you say "watch" you're waiting for the dog to look into your eye, as soon as they do, reward with the treat. Now repeat this at least ten times.

Tips

- Give breaks
- Clicker training makes your life easier
- Practice your hand gesture before commanding the dog
- Remember it takes time and patience

STEP 4

Enforcing eye contact

At this point the dog should be getting the gist. When the command "watch" is given, the dog should at this point be looking up at your eye. Now it is time to push the understanding. Take the food outwards away from your body. Try and get the dog to follow the hand with the treat. This is important for them to completely understand the command. At this moment as the dog is concentrating on the hand containing the food give the watch command. As this command is given the other hand gives the hand gesture like last time. The treat is given as soon as the dog looks back to your eye. Big reward is required at this moment. Repeat this step until you get ten reactions in a row.

Tips

- Say the command clearly.
- This step is a large milestone for the dog so their big reward should be you physically motivating them for the right behaviour.
- This can take time if the dog is struggling, go back to step 2.
- Breaks will be needed.

STEP 5

Eye to eye contact

Once you feel the dog has understood that the watch command requires eye to eye contact, try to prolong their stare up to 5 seconds. At this point you both are doing an amazing job, so do not forget to reward yourselves. At this stage you never reward the dog when they look away, only when they keep eye contact. We are aiming for this task now to become harder for both of you. The aim is now for the perfect watch command response.

Tips

- High reward
- Take breaks
- At this point you both are doing an amazing job, so do not forget to reward yourselves

STEP 6

Distraction training

Finally do this with distraction. Please do not rush at this point. It would be advisable to use small distractions at first such as toys and food being thrown; before moving on to other dogs, loud vehicles, or things in that nature. The aim is to have a large distraction going on around the dog whilst the dog is calmly looking up at you as you give the watch command. The key is to let the dog get distracted then give the command, if the dog is willing to listen to the command and ignore the surroundings you and the dog have mastered the watch command.

Tips

- Get creative and imagine what would benefit you in your local surroundings.
- High rewards are essential at this step.
- If you and your dog are struggling, it would be worth you both going back to step 2. Going back is a good thing, we do not want to rush this command.

This can be easily seen as one of the most important fundamental commands on this list of foundation tasks. In fact, this command should be the first one you master. Without this skill, you can't perform the rest correctly.

Walk Correctly

There are many ways to teach a dog to **walk correctly**. We are going to start with the checking system which is effective when done right. This system can be very effective for even the most difficult dogs. This is something that must be shown in person and not something that can be shared on paper. Which means if you are wanting to learn this method, please contact your local dog trainer. If this system is misunderstood, it can lead to the dog being mistreated in the process. You must acknowledge it is better to contact a local dog trainer if you want to learn this method for your dog.

Another technique which can be just as effective to solve walking issues is described below. The good thing about this training technique is that it is takes longer for the dog to master it. Therefore, the dog gets a better chance of understanding what you are wanting from them. This technique involves the human handler turning in on the dog and turning away whilst walking. This method requires patience and timing and should never be rushed.

Whilst a dog has been given the command "walk", the following rules are applied:

1. Never pull on the lead for any reason
2. Never let the dog sniff without permission
3. Keep the dog on one side, unless told otherwise
4. The dog must maintain a speed the handler has chosen (please take in the dog's ability)
5. No barking unless commanded
6. Trust the handler

These rules again must never be broken or rushed.

STEP 1

Start off with collar and lead

Firstly, we need to have chosen a side the dog needs to walk on. It can be transferable as the dog has to learn how to walk correctly on both sides of the handler. So, we will start with the left side in this written description.
Start slowly and step off with the dog on your left. Give the command "Walk" as you do so. The lead should be always loose (showing a U shape). Keep in mind that getting a perfect U shape in the lead takes time.

Tips

- Be space aware
- Collar and lead required
- No choke leads
- Speak clearly
- Do not rush these steps

STEP 2

Turning in on the dog

During this step it is important we get the movements right. **At no point should the dog be harmed in the process.** Now the idea is to walk back in the direction we came after about 4-5 steps. You begin the turn by moving your left leg out in front of the dog and then swing around to face the opposite direction. You can use your left leg to **gently guide (do not kick the dog)** the dog back onto your left side. It will take a bit of practicing, but this should be done in one smooth motion. **The guided dog** at this point should be facing the direction you have turned towards. So now you and the dog should be facing the other direction. Now we repeat this process once you have taken another 4-5 steps.

Tips

- For the first few times, don't worry about the lead having a U shape. However after repeating the process the dog will understand, it is easier to watch you and focus on you whilst they are walking.
- Practice the turn without the dog first. Allow yourself to get the movement and rhythm
- We are getting the dog to understand the idea of the exercise.
- We are guiding the dog.
- If the dog naturally looks up at you whilst performing the steps, use you voice to illustrate you are happy with their behaviour.
- Walk at your normal speed, do not rush your movements

STEP 3

Turning out on the dog

Now we are progressing on to more instructions for the dog. This time whilst walking we want to give the command "Walk". Repeat this command after making 4-5 steps. This time you turn the dog outwards. As you can image this task is easier. Remember that the aim is to guide the dog whilst they turn around. This move is more effective when the turn is done on the spot by the handler. These two movements should be repeated until you are smooth and seamless.

Tips

- Practice the turn without the dog first. Allow yourself to get the movement and rhythm
- The idea is for them to start associating the command with the action that follows.
- Your movement with the dog should flow, that is when you know you are ready to move on.

STEP 4

Repeating and rewarding

Now mix it up. Randomly choose from the two turns shown and remember to try increasing the number of steps between them after every turn. The most important thing to remember is to **change the direction as soon as the dog pulls on the lead.** Use sharp movements as you turn. It is also important not to forget to give the walk command. Let them know exactly what you want from them. Maintain this until the dog is focused on you and understands you are directing the walk.

Tips

- Change the pattern from using turning out or in.
- Take breaks after constant success.
- Reward often.
- Keep using the command "Walk".
- Record yourself, to make improvement.
- Go back to step 2 or 3 if you struggle at this point. Remember not to rush the dog through these steps.

STEP 5

Add distraction

We are about to do this with distraction. However, before we do this, we need to keep up the changing direction technique, but alter our speed. Go really slow then pick up the pace. We are wanting the dog to keep to your pace. Now after going up and down with speed change 10 times without issue, we can move on to adding in distraction. It is important to start with small distractions first like toys, food on the floor nearby and other people they know. After this has been mastered add more distracting challenges like other dogs, other people calling their name and high energy around them. If your dog cannot do this, please push on and keep trying. It might be worth going back to step 2 and revisiting the basics.

Tips

- Prep for this step.
- Imagination is key.
- Don't be worried to go back to the step 2.
- Do not rush these steps.
- You have done well so far.

STEP 6

Act like a baby treat like a baby

If you have got this far, well done. It is important to remember dogs will see what they can get away with especially whilst walking. Now it is time to take this out into the real world. Remember the phrase Act like a baby treat like a baby. Which means go back to square one. It is them who has got to learn at this point not you. So, give them a chance to make mistakes and change their direction. Then reward them when they are doing well. Dogs will try to keep breaking the rules. So, we take them back to step 1 and go again. The reason we do this is for the dog, allow the chance to understand the process and get a clear understanding what we the handler are asking of them. Remember training takes time and keeping strong is vital for the dog's success. Which is why maintaining the strict rules whilst walking is a must.

Tips

- Dogs in general love to use their nose especially on walks, therefore use this as a reward for walking nicely. But it is important we verbally command them to allow them to sniff.
- Going back to step 1 or 2 is a good thing as it allows the dog more time to learn.

Remember if your trained dog decides they have forgotten the training we start over again from the beginning. **They act like a baby we treat them like a baby**.

It is also important to have a command for when the dog is let off the lead. A command that lets the dog know it can relax and play. I would advise the command "play". A clear instruction lets the dog know that you have given them permission to play and enjoy itself.

Sit

This is probably the most well used and well-known command. However, it still needs to be performed perfectly. This command allows us as dog owners and trainers to engage with the dog and get them focusing on us. It is also a command that keeps a dog stationary, which can have its benefits in particular situations.

STEP 1

Advising and setting up the dog

Now with your treat encourage the dog to lick your hand. Your hand meanwhile needs to be clamped shut containing the treat. At this point the dog is focused on the treat. Positively encourage the dog to go backwards.
After that is successful, lift the hand up directing her or his bum to make contact with the ground. As soon as the dogs rear touches the ground reward the dog with the treat and with vocal praise. It's more effect when vocal praise is given all the way through.

Tips

- The dog should be kept on the lead throughout this training process
- This task will require treats (food motivation).
- Take each step slowly

STEP 2

Giving instruction

Repeat the process from step 1 and then start giving a command "sit". Remember only give the command once, don't confuse the dog by over repeating your words.
After a few attempts the dog should be getting the gist and going into a sit position.

Tips

- Do not use emotion in your command, irrelevant of if the dog is not understanding the task.
- Stop and go back to step 1.
- Take it slow.

STEP 3

Following your lead

Now we need to develop this newly learnt trick. Stand in front of the dog and bring them in towards you. The dog should be directed towards your knees. At this point give the command "sit", as soon as the command has been given bring the hand up guiding the dog into a flowing sit. Remember to reward the success.

Tips

- If the dog starts to struggle go back to step 1 and start again
- Might be worth practicing the movement first without the dog

STEP 4

Guidance with hand gestures

Repeat, repeat and repeat. Now repeat with no direct physical guidance. At this point the dog should know the sit command off by heart. If not go back to step 1 and start again. The next aim is to use hand signals.
We always want the dog looking at our eyes, showing us we have their attention. So, give the command "sit" whilst holding the treat in your clamped hand again. Shake it as if you are shaking your fist to your eye level. From this moment on the hand signal is performed every time you ask for a sit. After a few goes, I want you to say nothing and only give the hand gesture for a sit. The dog needs to do this without any verbal hints. Once this is achieved you can move onto the next step.

Tips

- Keep repeating until it becomes a natural movement for the dog
- Make this a joyful experience, remember this is meant to be fun.
- Never change your chosen hand gesture.

STEP 5

Final step

Congratulations your dog knows how to sit. At this point make it difficult for yourself, it is the only way you and your dog get better. Get a sit command from a long distance in a safe environment. Also get a sit at a random moment keeping the dog engaged and on its toes. Good luck.

Tips

- Keep this task fun

And remember if your trained dog decides they have forgotten the training we start over again from the beginning. **They act like a baby we treat them like a baby**.

Down

It goes without saying that the down is a fundamental technique to master. It is a command that is commonly used in more complex training tasks. It also has various useful day to day uses for example, getting the dog to stop whilst you check out a situation on a walk.

Whilst going through these steps below please maintain and keep the same word and hand gestures. This will stop any confusion whilst your dog is learning the commands given to them.

STEP 1

Introducing what we are wanting

For this training session we are going to need treats. Like previously mentioned getting a dog to work for their deeds is a great way to keep your dog engaged. We need to get the dog engaged with the food in the clamped hand again just as we did in the beginning of the sit command. Whilst we get the dog to engage with the hand, make sure the dog is licking and not biting.

Tips

- A clamped hand is where a treat is in the palm of the hand whilst the fingers cover it, in a fist like structure
- Food rewards required
- Allow time for the dog to understand and not to bite the hand.

STEP 2

Starting the engagement

Once you have the dog engaged with your hand, now it is time to get the dog's head to follow the hand containing the food. Hold your hand out in front of the dog. When they engage with the hand then slowly move your hand down towards the floor in front of their feet. The aim is for the dog to follow where the hand goes without chasing it, we want a controlled movement. At this stage the dog should be bent over licking the hand.

Tips

- Don't rush your movements
- Ensure the dog is enjoying the process

STEP 3

Follow on from step 2

Carrying on from step 2. Now directly move the hand towards them, as you do this your hand should already be near to the ground. This should get the dog to lower their bum to the ground and so achieve a down position. It's also okay at this stage to give them light encouragement by gently guiding their bum downwards with your hand to put the dog into a down. But at first please do wait and see if they can manage it without your assistance.
As soon as the dog goes into the down position stop and reward. Remember this is a big deal, so show it to them.

Tips

- Repeat the process
- Slow and steady, will make your life easier
- After a few successes, make it into a rhythm

STEP 4

Repeating the command

Now repeat this process a few times. However, this time command whilst your dog goes into a down. "Down" needs to be said in a joyful manner. I would advise doing this at least 10 times perfectly in a row before moving on. Really get the dog to understand the command.

Tips

- Command needs to be clear
- Only accept the perfect down
- You and your dog are doing an amazing job, do not forget to let your dog know this.

STEP 5

The hand gesture

Now we are going to see if they understand the "down" command. Remember if the dog is not able to complete this stage you must go back to step 2 and start again. So, we start step by step to make sure we have the dog's attention. This time we do not guide the dog to the floor. Just say "down" whilst giving a hand gesture. The hand gesture will consist of the index finger pointing as if you were pointing at someone. Now take that pointing finger and start doing a down motion whilst you give the command "down". At this point the dog should go into a down. This will require a high reward from you when achieved. If the dog is not able to complete this task, please repeat the last few steps; if the dog does achieve this task repeat it at least 10 times in a row.

Tips

- Repeat as much as you can
- Remember to break every 5 mins.
- This is a hard milestone. Please take this into account.

STEP 6

Commanding whilst distracted

Well done for getting to this point. Now we are going to allow the dog to wander around in a controlled space. Once the dogs mind has been distracted, get the dog's attention. Then give the command with the hand gesture. You should be able to do this at random intervals 10 times in a row. It is important to remember we need the dog to really understand that the hand gesture is part of this command.

Tips

- Maintain the hand gesture and keep the same

STEP 7

No words

Now only give the hand gesture. Do not give a verbal command. As soon as the dog goes into a down without you having to say anything you know you have mastered the down. Always make sure the hand gesture is clear and easy to see as this will allow the dog to understand what you are wanting. Keep the training up and well done.

Tips

- Please remember other species like horses can get intimidated when a dog is in a down position
- Each time a dog passes a step they need to receive a high reward, make the dog feel good and they will want to learn.

Remember if your trained dog decides they have forgotten the training we start over again from the beginning. **They act like a baby we treat them like a baby**.

Bed

First port of call is to understand how we can use this command. It's a positive way to express a timeout or a tool that can be used in day-to-day life, such as a command that stops a dog begging during dinner time.

This is a common form of training used by dog trainers. Therefore, you might hear other commands used that ultimately conclude the same results. The command is often called "place"; however, I feel more comfortable using "bed" due to it being translatable for most clients/dog owners.

The key training equipment that is required for this task is the raised training platform, abbreviated as TP in the below table. This often-square shaped platform can be purchased online or at your local pet shop. There are different sizes depending on the dog breed and their requirements.

It is worth getting a size which allows the dog in question to move around upon it, allowing them to get comfortable. These raised training platforms are often about 15 centimetres off the ground allowing the dogs to easily move on and off. This raised training platform is a great tool to allow the dog to deeply understand the bed command, which makes our job easier when converting into other locations once mastered on the training platform.

STEP 1

Bring in the raised training platform (TP)

Firstly, place TP before the dog is in the room. After this has been achieved, we bring the dog in the room and ignore the platform. Just play with the dog. Encourage the dog by using their name once in a positive manner then cuddle and play. During this play let the dog know you have treats to hand. Then suddenly stop your interaction with the dog, don't be negative just stop. The objective is to get the dog to relax and start wandering around the room/space. Your job at this moment is to quietly observe the dog as it wanders around. You are waiting for the dog to show interest in the platform. As soon as the dog shows interest, give a positive response to encourage the dog to come over to you and take a treat. Repeat this process at least 10 times before moving on.

Tips

- Don't rush the dog we do not want them to be fearful of the TP.
- Longer it takes for them to respond the better they will learn
- Once the TP is touched, use positive excitement as a reward, really get the dog to enjoy itself
- Don't move TP when the dog is on it ever. They need to trust it.
- Remember this training can take time

STEP 2

The brave first paw

Keep repeating the technique until you feel the dog is comfortable with the platform being in the room. Now get the dog to put a paw on the TP. I find if dogs are forced to go on the TP by lead, they will reject the command and you will find it hard to get them to complete the command. So, encourage the dog to step onto the TP, by having the treat in a clamped hand allowing the dog to lick the hand. This will allow the dog to focus on your hand whilst stepping on the platform. Whilst the dog is stepping up onto the TP use the command "bed" once. At the point the dog puts their paw on the TP, a massive reward is given. **This is a big deal for them.**

Tips

- Don't ever move TP once dog is on it
- Clamped hand means a hand in the shape of a fist. Stop if the dog bites you and start again
- Rushing this step can cause the dog to lose focus

STEP 3

Two paws on the TP

Now do the same process, to get two paws on the TP. Give the command and start to point to the TP as you do it.

Tips

- Don't ever move TP once dog is on it
- The dog should be understanding the process, in some cases the dog will perform natural improvements such as stepping on to the platform. It's important we encourage this behaviour

STEP 4

All paws on the TP

This time we are going to try and get all four paws on the TP. And get the dog to be comfortable on the TP. Repeat until it becomes instantaneous for the dog. And if you really want to push it try and get the dog to do bed just by pointing to the TP.

Tips

- The dog should be getting the gist by now, if not go back to step 2 and start again.

STEP 5

Commanding a sit and down

Right, you have got to step 5. At this point you should be feeling very proud of the dog. Add more commands whilst the dog is on the TP. Like sit and down, please look back to those sections to refresh your knowledge if needed. Also do not forget the hand signals that go along with them.

Tips

- It's good to make training difficult, this allows the dog to truly understand what we want from them as trainers

STEP 6

Walking around the dog on the TP. Keeping the dog on TP.

Well done. Now you and your dog are really going to push the limits. The aim of this section is to give the command "bed" and teach the dog to stay put. If you require a new hand signal to get the dog to stay on the TP, then do it. Once the dog is staying on top of the TP, start to make it more difficult by moving around the dog which should tempt the dog to break its position. We start small, therefore reward the dog from 30 seconds and work up from there. Do not forget the dog's attention span is 5 minutes, therefore whilst in training do not exceed that time.

Tips

- Give your dog a 5-minute training session then a 5- minute break (repeat this off and on process)
- Speak clearly with your commands
- **The dog is allowed to move around on the TP whilst you are walking around them, the idea is the dog does not come off the TP.**

STEP 7

Using the command on other beds in the house and outside

Your dog has done brilliantly. Now is the fun part. This should now be easy to translate to other bed items, such as blankets and mats. Remember hand signals and positive reactions make your life easier.

Tips

- Confidence is key. The dog needs to trust you

And remember if your trained dog decides they have forgotten the training we start over again from the beginning. **They act like a baby we treat them like a baby.**

Heel

This is probably the most show off task out of all the commands in the basic section. However, it is a basic command for a reason. This command is an important lesson for the dog about following your lead especially in situations that require your dog to be controlled. For example, on a walk and meeting a cyclist or aggressive dog. Getting your dog to walk to heel gives you the ability of control whilst moving away from the issue. It also gives the dog the ability to trust you as well. The knowledge that you as the leader would never walk them anywhere that would cause harm or discomfort to the dog.

We will also be using a hand gesture in this training session. The idea is to be able get the dog to focus and walk beside you without a verbal command given, only a hand gesture. The hand gesture is two fingers (your index and middle finger) pointing down to the floor by your hip.

STEP 1

Introduction to the task

To start this lesson, we need the right tools - a short lead that is attached to the dog's collar. Like most training techniques there are many methods of reaching the goal so please bear that in mind. This method has been chosen due to it often taking longer for the dog to learn which will give the dog a better understanding to what we want from them. Firstly, we choose a side, the side does not matter because once we have progressed with one side, we will repeat the technique on the other. As we need to illustrate what to do, the next step will start the exercise on the right-hand side, however you do not have to do this.

Tips

- Do not use an extendable lead for this task. It will make your life difficult.
- Treats will be required as a reward.
- Do not use a harness

STEP 2

Getting started

We are starting with the right side. Have the dog standing or sitting in front of you. From this position guide your dog with a treat reward. With the food in the right hand, guide your dog to your right side. Hold the treat in front of the dog then move your arm in a circle movement from in front of them, out to your side and then in close to your right hip. By moving your arm in this way, the dog should follow the treat and end up on your right-hand side and facing forwards. After completing the circle motion give the command "heel" and release the treat whilst giving the hand gesture next to your hip. Repeat this multiple times and only move on the other side once the dog is moving more confidently.

Tips

- Using the lead with the other hand is okay at this point.
- Start this task off with a positive energy

STEP 3

Guidance

We now want to give the command to the dog before we get them moving. Use the command "Heel" and this time guide them around to your right side by using the lead. Still have the treat in your hand and only release it once the dog is in the correct position on your side and you have given the hand gesture. It is important that you repeat this until the dog is doing the movement without much or any guidance from the lead. Once this behaviour is recurring then mirror the methods on the left side.

Tips

- Remember you are supposed to be inviting. Make it a friendly experience. We want them to feel safe in this position.

STEP 4

Dropping the lead

It is now time to drop the lead and guide them using your hand movements and treats. After repeating the command give them less and less guidance with your hands as you go on. Keep going until you are only saying "heel" and giving a hand gesture. Once this happens on both sides at least five times in a row move on the next step. Don't forget high rewards are given at this point.

Tips

- Make sure you are in a safe environment
- Take the movement slowly, rushing will cause confusion
- Build your confidence slowly

STEP 5

Taking the first steps

At this point the dog should understand the command by now. Therefore, we need to move on. Give the command and hand gesture, as soon as the dog finds itself in line with your leg, step off whilst giving another command and reward. Repeat it again and increase the number of steps every time. Make sure the dog has kept itself in line with your leg before giving the reward. The final aim of step 5 is to move five steps forward with the dog perfectly in line with you. Remember to do this on both sides.

Tips

- Make sure you in a safe and controlled environment

STEP 6

Walking up and down

By this point the dog should know what side heel is wanted by observing the hand gesture given at the time. So, we will be putting this to the test. Have your dog sitting in the distance and recall them into a heel. From the chosen side, walk the dog with a dropped lead up and down always keeping the dog on the chosen side. I would suggest using a treat for this task. Remember to give the command "heel" whilst you walk up and down and keep your hand gesture steady. Once this has been mastered on both sides, do it again with a small distraction. Make it harder as you go.

Tips

- Remember clear voice instruction

STEP 7

Taking what we know to the real world

Now it is the time we have been waiting for. To show off your dog's ability to heel. I would advise using this in an area with large spaces like a public field. However, please do keep the dog on lead until you are confident you have control of the dog. Always push the boundaries and get the dog to understand that a high reward always follows a heel command that has been given and performed correctly.

Tips

- Having control of your dog is important. As it is a legal requirement for all dogs in the UK to be always under control
- If you feel like the dog needs more training please go back to the previous steps, there is no shame in ensuring you are ready

And remember if your trained dog decides they have forgotten the training we start over again from the beginning. **They act like a baby we treat them like a baby.**

Recall

It goes without saying that recall training is important for all dogs and their owners. Health and safety circles around your ability to recall your dog, knowing that your dog will listen to you and come back to you in any situation.

Whilst we do this training, we need to remember that a dog wants to investigate the world around them. Due to their inquisitive nature we need to understand that we can easily become considered as boring, compared to an outdoor environment full of amazing smells. When given a choice, the dog might not always choose you. Therefore, training the recall which means returning to you every time when called upon, is essential. Another important factor to remember is that the recall should not involve the dog's name. This is as a precaution so that the dog's name is never used in a negative way, as this can lead to the dog forming a negative association to their own name. Instead, use commands such as "come", "feet", "here" or "to me". All these commands are simple and easy to say quickly, which is wise when letting your dog off lead.

STEP 1

Preparation

This is a command that needs to be always said clearly and confidently. The dog's name is not used during this command. I would recommend the command "feet", due to it being quick to say and most importantly it will not be used in another meaning.
So, for this training exercise you will require a long training lead (the longer the better) and open space. Additionally, you will also require food treats as a reward.

Tips

- Choose an environment that is easy to control - minimise the distractions
- If you do not use the command "feet", you can choose another word. However, remember that you will not be able to change it from here on. We do not want to confuse the dog

STEP 2

Understand the command

At this point you should be ready. Firstly, wait until the dog is distracted. Allow them to sniff around and lose their concentration on you. In the beginning it is recommended to start off with a short distance. The next actions are important to follow. Whilst holding the lead, give the command "feet ", at this moment take three steps backwards then go down on one knee. Remember to be vocally positive during this to encourage the dog to come over. The aim is to get the dog as close as possible to you. Keeping the treat held close to your stomach allows you control of the dog. This needs a high reward response, let the dog know how happy you are with them.

Tips

- Being enjoyable and energetic will encourage better results from your dog.
- Timing is everything when giving rewards.
- Keep the action consistent.
- The command and learning work best when you show enjoyment in the tasks.

STEP 3

Our foot work

Repeat this process again and again then slowly increase the distance on the training lead. It is not uncommon at this point that the dog can start delaying their response to the given command and can start losing focus. To help get the focus back, once the "feet" command is given jolt the lead lightly to refocus their attention. It is important that the jolt is very soft and light, aim for movement of the lead that would occur if a small bird, such as a sparrow, landed on the lead. Remember when it comes to distance, don't be worried about going back to short distance. We need the dog to understand the process.

Tips

- Remember to always have control of your dog.
- Do not get lazy and remain consistent as the dog will learn your boundaries and will adapt to your arm reaching distance, therefore always reward close to your stomach.
- Only reward when it is perfect.

STEP 4

Allow to wander

At this point the dog in training should be starting to understand the process. Now keep the dog on the long lead, allow the dog to start wandering in the open space. Wait until the dog has focused on something in the space. As soon as the dog's attention has been taken, give the lead a soft and light tug like we discussed earlier and give the recall command. Once again performing the same foot work. You want to repeat this with different distancing and at random times. A good way to know if you are ready for the next step, is to be able to get a perfect recall without tugging the lead 10 times in a row.

Tips

- Please use light tugging. It is just to get the dogs attention. Hurting a dog does not achieve anything, we want the dog to enjoy the activity.
- Do a pattern of 5 minutes of training and 5 minutes of break
- Do not rush this step, give the dog the opportunity to learn

STEP 5

Bigger and better distraction

Congratulations for getting to step 5. The dog by now should have a good understanding of the command. Whilst the dog is still on the long lead, we will start adding distractions, such as favourite toys or new people, into the training space. Allow the dog to get distracted by them and then get a perfect recall. We are looking for the dog to stop and immediately come to you, allowing you to have control of their movements. One of the best distractions is another person, allowing them to play with the dog for a few minutes. Then give the recall command. The person playing needs to stop interacting at this moment. The dog should respond with a perfect recall. If this does not happen, this means that the dog needs to go back to step 2 and re-learn. Otherwise repeat this recall to get 5 perfect recalls in a row.

Tips

- With the distractions, start off small and slowly get bigger.
- Take a break every 5 minutes

STEP 6

Lose the lead

Like step 5 we are looking to use distractions in our controlled open space. Please remember the space should be secure to prevent the dog from running off whilst we are still training. After that has been confirmed please let the dog off lead. We are going to do the same things as in step 5 but this time the dog is going to be off lead. Remember please go back to step 2 if the dog stops responding.

Tips

- If this is not your 5th day of training recall you are rushing this command too quickly.
- Prolonging training methods allows the dog to understand the technique better.

STEP 7

Taking the dog into the real world

Taking the dog out into the real world requires common sense. Remember as the owner or guardian of the dog you are responsible. Therefore, it might be worth using a long lead during your first couple of goes. Think carefully about the environment you are letting them off in. For example, doing it in a location where your dog has access to a road would not be suitable.

Tips

- Know your dog's abilities and slowly push their boundaries
- Remember you are now in a public area, and you are responsible for your dog's actions.
- Know and respect the law when it comes to dogs in public areas
- Always keep you voice positive and welcoming when recalling the dog

And remember if your trained dog decides they have forgotten the training we start over again from the beginning. **They act like a baby we treat them like a baby**.

Wearing a muzzle

Why does my dog need to learn to wear a muzzle? Well, this is a good question. A muzzle does not have to be a bad thing, it just provides the owner with the ability to control their dog. The idea that a dog wearing a muzzle means the dog is a dangerous and aggressive dog is wrong. There are many reasons why a dog wears a muzzle such as the dog likes to eat poo whilst on a walk. If your dog is comfortable with you putting a muzzle on them, it shows they have great trust in you as their owner.

This training technique can lead to distrust and confusion from the dog. Therefore, the steps given must be done slowly and correctly so do not rush this technique.

STEP 1

Start off slowly

Please remember the slower you do these steps, the better the outcome will be. We do not want the dog to become scared of the muzzle. We must get them to trust us and the muzzle. Therefore, telling the dog off is a big no during this task.

Now it is time to firstly introduce the muzzle by bringing the muzzle into the environment, you may leave it on the floor or hold it if you wish. Do not put the muzzle near the dog's mouth unless they want to interact with it. Please remember you should never be putting the muzzle over its mouth at this stage.

Tips

- Try your best to get the right size without putting in on their face.
- Don't rush. Always do it in the dog's time.
- Once you have the muzzle in the room, interact with your dog as you normally would and ignore the muzzle.

STEP 2

Muzzles are fun to be around

Now hold the muzzle in your hand and play a game with your dog. Do not use the muzzle as a toy, the muzzle is just present when the dog is having fun. This lets the dog know that when the muzzle comes out, they are about to have fun.

Tips

- Do this for a few days
- Don't rush

STEP 3

Make the muzzle tasty

The dog should now be aware that the muzzle comes out when good things happen. Remember not to rush these steps. Now it is time to use a dog friendly spreadable treat, such as squeezable cheese, on the rim of the muzzle and allow the dog to lick it off. The dog should not take the muzzle off you or chew on the muzzle.

Tips

- Do this step for a few days
- Speak to the dog in a soft positive voice throughout this step

STEP 4

Head into the muzzle

Now put the cheese paste in the muzzle. Allow the dog to lick the paste out of the muzzle in its own time, whilst you hold the muzzle securely. Do not put the strap on the dog. Repeat this step as many times as possible.

Tips

- Keep your hand steady, allowing the dog to trust you

STEP 5

Muzzle starting to stay on

After repeating the previous step many times, the dog will be ready for this step once the dog quickly puts his head into the muzzle without hesitation. This shows the dog trusts you. At this stage put a small amount of cheese paste into the muzzle and hold onto the cheese paste tube. Once the dog puts their head into the muzzle, start to feed small amounts through the muzzle. After repeating this at least 10 times, the dog should understand the relationship between muzzle and food. Now it is time to tie up the straps and keep feeding small amount of cheese. Only leave the straps on for a few seconds at a time. And slowly build up to two minutes. This can take days to be achieved. However, if the dog rejects the muzzle start from step 2 again.

Tips

- Make sure you observe the dog's behavioural displays, the dog will be talking to you with their body language
- Do not rush the dog
- This is a delicate process

STEP 6

Distraction

The dog at this point should be allowing the muzzle to be on for at least 2 minutes or more. Now as soon as you put on the muzzle, I want you quickly go into a play with the cheese paste. The muzzle needs to stay on whilst you are playing and interacting. If the dog tries to get the muzzle off, try to distract them as much as you can. As soon as the dog is distracted and has forgotten about the muzzle, take off the muzzle. Keep repeating the exercise and slowly finish off with the muzzle being left on. Any time the dog starts to fight the muzzle, stop quickly and restart from step 2.

Tips

- Break every 5 minutes

STEP 7

Your own mind set

Now go and play with the dog whilst they have the muzzle on. The dog should be comfortable. Their mind set thinks this is something not to be concerned about. **Don't worry about other people's perceptions, the dog doesn't.** But remember if the dog at any point starts to reject the idea, start training back at step 1 again as the dog will need to be retrained in this entire process.

Tips

- If you feel you do not currently have any need to use a muzzle, that is fine. It is best to place the muzzle on the dog at least once a week to maintain the training. This means the dog should be comfortable wearing a muzzle if you do need to use one at some stage.

And remember if your trained dog decides they have forgotten the training we start over again from the beginning. **They act like a baby we treat them like a baby.**

Next step of training

Please **do not jump** to this section without mastering the basic commands. You are only doing the dog and yourself injustice. The basic commands are fundamental to learning the more advanced commands. Additionally, they will also help build a strong relationship between you and your dog allowing you to perform more advanced tasks together.

You will find that a lot of the basic commands are needed to perform these advanced training techniques. A lot of the advanced techniques are quite often taught with the use of equipment, such as choke collars or easy-walker harnesses, and these often provide a short-cut or quick fix to the problem. However, the methods you will learn limits the use of these type of training tools as it is important that the dog truly understands what you are wanting from them. Whereas using a quick fix can lead to dogs misunderstanding the lessons brought to them.

Control barking

A command that is liked by the neighbours. A good dog should be allowed to inform the household when people are approaching the home. If the dog is always under control by you, it's a job they will happily provide with little training. It is probably best to understand the methodology behind this technique before beginning. The idea of this training method is to get the dog to bark more so that we as the owner or trainer can control it. Once we can command the dog to bark, we can then control the barking and therefore stop them from barking when it becomes undesirable. We do not want the dog to stop barking all together as it is a dog at the end of the day.

STEP 1

Setting the environment

We need to make sure we have the right space and equipment. The most important part of the training session is the location. We need a place that we can tie the dog up to. The place the dog is tied up to needs to be able to hold the dog's weight as we are going to want the dog to pull. Now attach a lead to the chosen location.

Tips

- Choose a location that allows you to control the distractions
- Do not rush these steps
- Ensure the dog sees the treats as a high value reward

STEP 2

Beginning steps

Now we bring the dog to the location and put them on the lead which is tied up to the steady object mentioned in step 1 **(never leave the dog whilst they are tied up at any point, they must always see you)**. We want the dog to be energized and excited to do this task. When they are tied up for the first time give them a positive interaction like a cuddle or something in that nature.

Tips

- Make sure the structure can hold the dog's weight
- Make sure you know what gets a reaction from your dog that you can control

STEP 3

Encouraging barking

Now we are going to encourage the dog to bark. We are going to do this by getting the dog excited which should get the dog to bark. As soon as the dog barks the first-time, reward with a food treat immediately. Repeat this a few times. Only move on once the dog understands when they bark it results in them being rewarded.

Tips

- Practice your timing
- High energy can be used at this stage

STEP 4

Timing the command

As you have reached this step, the dog should understand that barking results in a treat being given. Now as the dog barks, we are going to give a command "speak" then give them the reward. Repeat this at least 10 times until they understand "speak" is related to barking and the reward given.

Tips

- Practice your timing
- Speak clearly
- Do not rush the dog

STEP 5

Asking for the command

Now we are going to be firm and stubborn with the dog. Give the command "speak" and wait for the dog to bark. Wait until the dog responds. Do not reward until the dog gives you what you want. As soon as you receive a bark after the command is given, a high reward is required. Repeat this process until you get 10 requested barks in a row.

Tips

- Reward immediately when the dog barks after the command is given
- Timing is everything
- Ignore all unrequested barking
- At this point we will require time and patience from you the trainer

STEP 6

The differences

Now the dog needs to know they are only going to be rewarded if the bark has been requested by you. So, if you get a bark without giving the command the dog should receive a firm "no". However, please remember to go into a positive state after you say no to prevent a negative association from forming.Keep repeating and reacting positively to barks that have commanded. Do this until the dog clearly understands the response required for the command "speak".

Tips

- This will take time for the dog to understand
- Do not rush the dog
- Go back to step 1, if the dog starts to struggle with the task

STEP 7

How do we use this in everyday life

The dog at this point should understand by now what you expect from them. If not, please start from step one. If the dog is clearly understanding the training, then we need to make sure we use this command daily. It is important to reinforce the idea that you control when the dog barks. Remember to lightly discipline if an unwanted bark occurs with a verbal “no”. Then change it into a positive experience as soon as the discipline moment is over.

Tips

- A happy and healthy dog should be asked to bark at least once a day to prevent frustration

Stay/wait

This command becomes easier when all the basic commands are learnt first. Again, hand gestures are important for the task to be performed correctly.

Please note your dog will be performing some of the basic commands within these steps, therefore make sure your dog can perform them before doing this task. There are many words we can choose. A commonly used word is "holt" which is a French word used to stop movement. This is also a great command which is neutral as it is difficult to attach emotion to its pronunciation.

Remember when you choose a word you need to stick with it.

STEP 1
Setting in early hand gestures

Begin in a space and environment we can control. We want as few distractions as possible. First, ask the dog to sit. Please remember to use the appropriate hand gesture for this command. Now we are wanting to use the command "holt". At this moment you need to provide a hand gesture. Even though the dog will not understand it for now, it better to start the hand gesture off early. Use the gesture of your hand held flat out as if you were commanding a stop. Once your dog has stayed still for a few seconds, give a treat and fuss. Repeat this a few times before moving on the step 2.

Tips

- Give one command after the other, ensuring you're not blending each task together as this would cause confusion to your dog

STEP 2
Extending the wait

At this stage we are still asking for a sit before the command of "holt" is used. We are still using hand gestures as we were in step one, but this time try and extend the dogs wait to 5 seconds. If at any point the dog breaks, restart the steps from the beginning. Repeat this at least ten times.

Tips

- Remember to take breaks.
- Do not rush this step
- Making this step a positive experience will make the rest of the steps easier

STEP 3
Creating more distance

At this point the dog should be understanding the process. Now from the sit position give the command to stay once more with the hand gesture. Leave the hand gesture out in front of you and take one step backwards repeat the command "holt". The best advice I can give you is to take the backward step slowly. If the dog stays, quickly step in and reward the good behaviour. Repeat.

Tips

- Don't rush your foot work
- Ensure the dog is always watching you

STEP 4

Creating a rhythm

Now we are doing the same again but take more steps backwards. Gradually increase the distance between you and the dog. It's important when rewarding the dog, we always go to them. Never call them to you, this will destroy the process and aim of this command.

STEP 5

Enforcing the training ideas

At this point you should be able to move at least five meters away whilst the dog stays in its location. Now it's time to make it hard. Again, repeat the beginning process of getting into a sit and then into a stay. But this time keep the hand gesture out and slowly walk around the dog in a circle. Remember you may repeat the command "holt" but do not say it too often and say it with confidence as you make your way around the dog. If the dog continuously breaks and moves towards you, go back to step 1. It is important the dog understands what we are wanting from them. Always reward the dog as you both go further up the steps.

Tips

- Take your time and increase the distance slowly
- Speedy movements encourage dogs to come to you so take it slow

Tips

- Clear hand gestures
- Speak clearly
- Give the dog 5-minute breaks

STEP 6

Free roaming

We are going to let the dog move freely around the room or space. At any random point give the command "holt". You must expect the dog to stay still. The dog must be rewarded if they stay in their location. It doesn't matter if they stay standing, sitting or lying down. Repeat the process 5 times. The next stage is to keep them freely moving and give the command at a random point in time. We are looking for them to stay still for 30 seconds, whilst you randomly move around the room giving them the command to stay. Don't go more than 30 seconds.

Tips

- Give your dog time to freely move around the provided space. Keep the command unpredictable. This will help the dog's learning and listening ability.
- Say the command with confidence

STEP 7

Out in the open

Now it's time to take you dog outside on a large field and let them play. Randomly give the command and they should be able to instantly stop and stay where they are. If you can successfully repeat this process without any issue, you both have mastered this command. Well done.

Tips

- Keep finding ways to make this training harder, please always keep safety in mind.
- Remember you are responsible for your dog, therefore choosing a safe space is vital.

Scent training

Scent training is a task that all dogs will enjoy participating in. It allows them to turn an enjoyable past time into an activity that pleases you, the owner or trainer. It is quite easy to get the dog to enjoy this job role. Please take in account 30 minutes of scent training is equivalent of a 1 hour walk. Too much scent training in a day can fry the dog's mind.

Start off with a chosen scent. I would advise using one scent at first. In this case we are going to use sunflower oil, which is a great starting point for the dog. For this task we will use a Kong and an absorbent material such as toilet roll tissue. It is important to pick the correct size Kong to the size of your dog, for health and safety reasons. Inside this Kong you will want to put normal tissue which will soak up the oil and the smell. It is important that we do not let the dog eat the tissue. Again, it is all about control, so the basics need to be mastered before training scent work. Finally add the sunflower oil, the aim is to use just enough for the tissue to take in the scent before being overwhelmed by the volume.

Before we start it is important that we give a command that never changes, for obvious reasons. The advice would be to use the word "find" then the instruction of the desired object. For example, for the dog to search for sunflower oil we could say "find sunny". This instruction would mean the dog needs to find the specific object that you have requested. Another related example is teaching the dog to find the car keys, which would require an instruction of "find motor".

The words you say are not important if the command is clear and consistent. These are just guides that are easy to use and remember.

This can be transferred into anything you want. For example, you get the dog to search for lost money, keys, remotes, or phones. The possibility is limited only by you the trainer and your imagination.

STEP 1

Keeping to the word

Before we begin, we need to choose the word and stick with it. In this case we will be using "find sunny". Additionally, the Kong with the sunflower oil should already be prepped before we begin.

We start by bringing the Kong down to the dog's level. From here we want the dog interested in the Kong. As soon as the dog comes over to the Kong use the command "find sunny" and then immediately treat the dog. This process will need to be repeated at least 10 times in a row.

Tips

- Choose a location with few distractions
- Highly positive reactive reactions when the dog achieves each step
- Keep to the word
- This task will require treats

STEP 2

Getting to know the scent

The dog should now be happy to engage with the Kong. At this point let the dog come over to the Kong. Whilst holding onto the Kong, put it out in front of you. Allow the dog to come over and touch the Kong with their nose. Before you put the Kong out give a clear and energetic command "find sunny". The dog should come over to the Kong and smell it whilst touching it with their nose. As soon as this is achieved, a high reward is given. Make it energetic and exciting.

Tips

- Remember this task has got to be fun
- The dog should want to participate
- Highly positive reactive reactions when the dog achieves each step

STEP 3

Understand the steps

As we reach this step the dog should be reacting to the Kong as soon as you give the command. If not, the dog still needs time. Therefore, please repeat step 2 before going to step 3. This step is to give the dog further understanding. We first are going to get the dog to go into a down position. Now we will ask them to stay, then take a few steps backwards and place the Kong directly in front of your feet. At this point give the command "find sunny". Wait for the dog to come over to the Kong located by your feet. When the dog touches the Kong, immediately and positively pick up the Kong and get the dog to sit. When the dog is in a sit, give a high reward. Repeat this step until the dog automatically goes into a sit without asking.

Tips

- Give confident commands
- Only reward perfect reactions
- Do not rush this step
- This step can take a few days to be achieved

STEP 4

Placing the Kong

The dog should now understand more of what we are wanting from them. We are going to ask the dog to go down and stay in that position. This time we are going to place the Kong in a random place within the room that is within their view. Allow them to watch the entire process. Once the Kong is placed, step away from it and give the dog the command "find sunny". The dog should make a beeline for the Kong. We are wanting the dog to touch it with its nose or paw and sit down, if the dog is clearly instructing you that they have found the Kong they have achieved the task. The dog might still need assistance with sitting after locating the Kong. Please repeat this process until the dog locates it and sits. Place the Kong in a different location within the room each time. This stage will take a long time.

Tips

- Reduce the excitement at this stage, we want the dog under control
- Patience is needed as this will take a long time to perfect

STEP 5

Hide and go seek

At this point the dog should be able to go to the location of the Kong and sit as soon as the Kong has been located.
Now remove the dog from the training location. Once the dog has been removed and cannot see into the training location, place the Kong underneath an object like a cone. After the Kong has been hidden bring the dog back in. Get the dog to go down and stay. When you're happy to start, command the dog "find sunny". They will start to use their nose to find the Kong. Remember when the dog finds the Kong make sure the dog then sits. When this is achieved give a high reward. Keep repeating this process.

Tips

- Important to repeat your success
- Give your dog breaks, this can be a lot to take in

STEP 6

Making the task harder

The dog will now know the command "find sunny" and will be able to locate the scent even when the object/ Kong is hidden. This allows us to push the dog's ability to search and find the hidden Kong. Get creative and start to hide the Kong around the house and garden. Keep changing the location and allow yourself and your dog to have fun whilst scent training

Tips

- Have fun with this task, they will be more eager to find the location of the chosen scent
- Do not put the scent out of the dog's reach
- Give the dog time and allow them to make mistakes and head in the wrong direction

STEP 7

Final push

At this point we will be taking the dog outside of its own environment. It is important to know that the dog has perfect recall and other fundamental basic commands to keep them safe. Take the dog onto a field where wind blows and moves the scent to make the dog's life harder. Once you have chosen the location, hide the Kong slightly underground without the dog knowing and see whether the dog can find it or not. If the dog can repeatedly find the hidden Kong, you have both mastered scent training.

Tips

- Give the dog as much time as they need
- They will work out a strategy
- The harder the better
- Woods are also a fun place to perform scent training
- Please do not bury the Kong too deep. We would suggest a maximum depth of 3 inches deep

Get creative

It's time to make your own step by step training method. Your time to do something fun with your dog. That is why we got a dog right? To have a best friend to make memories with. Remember the training process will strengthen the bond you have with your dog; I am pretty sure you will agree it is worth it.

The dogs mind

Dogs have social systems built from respect and politeness. That's why it is important to start training and socializing dogs at a young age if you have the chance, this does not apply to you if your dog is a rescue. It is self-explanatory that you would not be able to control this factor if you are rehoming an adult dog.

Social systems can be observed by watching dogs in the park in a social environment. You will find the ones that keep getting themselves into trouble are being rude and not following the strict rules. In other words, they have not learnt their place. This is where you will find humans make the situation worse by making a problem where there isn't one. Especially when their young dog needs to learn how to socialize within the universal rules of dogs. These dogs need to learn that things like sniffing others without asking or being uncontrollably hyper will result in a vigilant older dog telling them off. My advice to those owners is to let it happen, most adult dogs are aware they are dealing with a puppy and will act accordingly. There are many components to dog's social interactive rules. One that seems to be the strictest is play. This is to ensure play does not turn into confrontation. Dogs that break these strict play rules will find themselves being isolated or not trusted by other dogs in the social community. The strict rules prevent the chance of physical play from being misunderstood and from leading into a fight situation, especially in a group setting. Please be aware most dogs do not want to fight and will also provide dog universal signs that they are unhappy with the situation.

Dogs learn all these behaviours by socializing with other puppies and being taught by older dogs around them. Therefore, if your young dog has been bitten on the ear by another dog they have met, they have just been given the nice option which teaches them to act more respectfully around other dogs.

Now we are going to get into detail about the commonly used phrase "being the alpha". This common phrase seems to be causing issues in the dog training community, with some trainers believing it is correct whilst others in the community believe it is an outdated thought process. There are scientific studies on stray/wild dogs that clearly show that there are pack structures, and these can be correlated to dogs that live together in the same domestic household. These research findings have confirmed that there is an alpha in a domestic dog's social structure, however humans have somehow twisted the idea of what an alpha is.

Firstly, it is important to note that dogs know that you are human, and that they are a dog. The social structures on how they react and behave to you are different.

When you hear the phrase "be the alpha/ leader" that is the correct terminology being used, in respect of dog training. Often, the dog trainer using the terminology will then highlight how you can present yourself as one. This often involves controlling a dog in a particular situation that will lead to the dog feeling more comfortable in letting you deal with the situation at hand. The dog should be confident in allowing you to take control of any situation as this is an essential attribute to have in today's world. Nowadays the idea of the alpha/ leader is an aggressive character that deals out punishment and never allows themselves to be fun and this is wrong.

There is an interesting study (Bonanni, R., Cafazzo, S., Abis, A., Barillari, E., Valsecchi, P. and Natoli, E., 2017. Age-graded dominance hierarchies and social tolerance in packs of free-ranging dogs. Behavioral Ecology, 28(4), pp.1004–1020) which illustrates a clear insight into dog pack hierarchy in domestic dogs when they are given the opportunity to exhibit more wild behaviours in a stray living situation. The study which this training manual urges you to read, discovers that dogs are more likely to follow an alpha that has a calm and controlled personality, and this seems to come with age in the domestic dog. The alphas in these stray packs would be the ones that knew where to find food and could control themselves in any situation. That is what makes an alpha in the dog's world, not the idea of a strong dog that could fight off all other dogs and would force it's will on the other dogs around them.

The findings from the study into the social structure of dogs backs up the idea which has been common knowledge; that these animals are able to live in a pack structure, although some breeds find this easier than others. However, it is worth reminding you that a dog is designed for their main function to be human companions, which in turn provides them a role. Humans can try to find out whether young puppies are going to be good working tools by performing dog behavioural testing called puppy testing. These are harmless tests carried out by various recognised organisations such as the police, army, canine assistant organisations and search and rescue. This will allow you to have the perfect working dog.

So, as you can see humans and dogs do not think the same way. Why people feel that a leader needs to be horrible to others to assert their control makes some dog trainers question our species' entire thinking process. These true alpha dogs are desirable by all trainers as a training tool, but unfortunately, they are not easy to come by.

Understanding dominance in dogs is worth knowing as previously mentioned as this can be exhibited differently depending on various factors. We have learnt that the size of the dog does not matter and it's their individual attitude that counts when it comes to pack structures. You might be wondering which factors determine where a dog will be placed in a pack structure. One example is gender, well dogs don't care about gender. A male can be in charge over a female and a female can be in charge over a male. This completely comes down to the individuals involved. However, it must be said, female dogs seem to be in charge more often when paired up with a male in a family setting. This could be because, based on previous experience, females are normally more level-headed than males. However, this is not scientifically proven and is based on experience only.

Now moving on to a different section of the dog's mind set. Trust is an important factor when it comes down to training and living with your dog. It is important to remember that if the dog does not trust you, that is your fault not the dogs. Even if the dog is a rescue, it is your responsibility to build that trust. Getting annoyed with them just makes it worse and makes your job harder. It is always easier said than done in most cases but give them time and go at their pace.

If you are confident and you have earned the dog's trust, you will notice these amazing animals will follow you anywhere. Dogs do not want to follow a leader who second guesses themselves or is not confident in situations. The dog notices anything you do and feel. For example, when someone rings a doorbell, you need to command the situation. The dog is **commanded** to go to bed or wait, whilst you the owner calmly deal with the door. It is about control and introducing a calm environment around you.

Another truth about the dog's mind is that all dogs have limitations in some training areas, which often comes down to individual personalities. Please do not misunderstand, they can be worked on through training, but there can be limitations to how much they can do. Which is like us humans. We can do most things when we learn and train, however we also have our limits in particular subjects. Therefore, owners just need to be aware of these limits so we don't harm our dogs. **You will never get the same dog twice.** People who have had the same breed of dog multiple times will know what this means. Which truly makes it more beautiful owning your very own dog. Therefore, it is pointless to compare your individual dog to other dogs whilst you are training them.

Figure 1: Domestic dog hierarchy structure

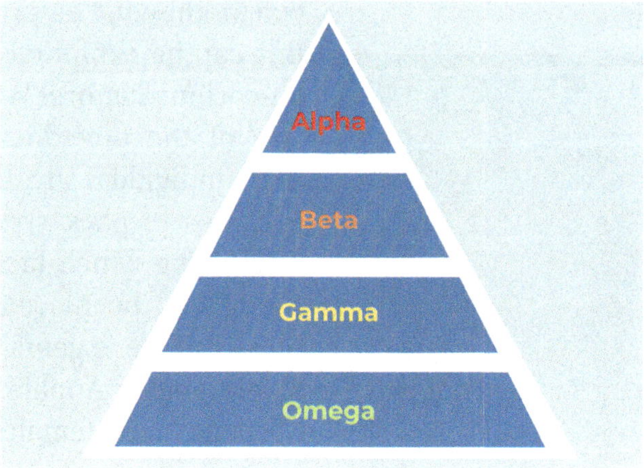

Continuing from explaining how dominance works, it is important to understand the social group structure. There are some trainers out there who do not believe in pack structures, which is fine. Therefore, please bare this in mind when speaking to your dog trainer.

Resources would suggest there is strong evidence that these animals have a pack structure. A lot of people would think that these pack structures are the same as a wolf pack structure. **This is not true**, domestic dogs and wolf species do not have the same rules in their pack structures. However, this does not mean these two species cannot communicate with each other, because they can. A dog and a wolf do have a few compatible social cues that will allow them to communicate with each other, for example the play bow.

The dog group structure is important for every dog, it allows them to know who is where and who needs to be listened to. However, pack structure can often change very quickly. This can be caused by different environments or situations. All this is often done without a single bit of violence or bloodshed. A single change in body language and behaviour can change a groups social structure.

You could be reading this manual because your dog has behavioural issues and are hoping there is information in here that could correlate specifically to your dog's issue. Well knowing your dog's mindset is key. It is better to perceive the world in the same way your dog does. For example, if your dog is anxious with people, it is likely they find human affection challenging. You should always keep that dog wanting more when it comes to human affection. Which is why forcing the affection and not allowing the dog to come to you in its own time can be equally damaging for dog's perception of human contact. Therefore, it is essential we know how to address this dog, especially when we show affection. **Cuddle the dog under the mouth, dogs are not keen on getting stroked on the top of the head.** This stroking method is essential if you have a nervous dog. Some of you reading this might think this is wrong as your dog enjoys a head stroke, this is due to some dogs being conditioned to like anything, and in some cases, loving being stroked on the head. It is worth keeping this in mind when meeting a strange new dog or dog showing signs of being nervous.

But the real solution to all undesirable behaviour is getting help. We all cannot be expected to know everything, so get in contact with a local dog trainer, they will get you started on the right track.

Harsh truth

Owning a dog is not a right, it's a privilege. A dog does not judge you as an owner, but other people will judge your actions. If you haven't got the time to walk your dog and do not want to pay anyone to do it for you, please ask yourself why you want a dog in the first place. The harsh truth is owning a dog requires you to provide them with stimulation and money as the expenses for things such as vet bills, food, toys, beds, etc. soon add up.

There is a breed out there for mostly everyone. A lot of people want a dog based on its looks but, they should pick a dog based on their needs and research. For example, if you want a dog to take on holiday during the summer and do hiking or walking into the countryside for a few days, a French Bulldog, Husky or Newfoundland is not for you. Huskies can suffer in the heat, even UK temperatures, if not looked after during hot spells. However, if you are thinking of hiking around Inverness in the winter period you have chosen the perfect dog.

When choosing the right breed for you, researching breed requirements and how to be a responsible dog owner is helpful. It can also be beneficial to get in touch with a local dog trainer as they might be able to show you examples and give you a personal experience which can point you in the right direction. Additionally, if you want to get in contact with companies such as Dog Academy Pro please do. Responsible dog ownership should always be rewarded and supported.

One question most first-time dog owner's ask themselves is "Should I even have a dog?" Well, if you are the sort of person who likes to scream at everything with excitement and has uncontrollable energy, it would be advisable to question yourself and see if are willing to change on behalf of your dog. Uncontrollable energy can cause behaviour issues which are often ignored and build up to a boiling point. Remember, dogs are great mirrors of their environment. If you conclude that a dog does not suit your lifestyle, remember there are other domesticated species out there that will suit your needs and requirements.

This is only said for the dog's sake, the truth is not something we want to hear. Dogs are fantastic animals and really do have complex emotions and feelings that are affected by human neglect. Please do not mistake that this training manual believes dogs cannot make our lives better, because they 100% can and will to the right owner. As potential owners we need to think about what the dog needs as well.

Let's finish this section on a positive note. What is the best type of dog owner?

The best type of dog owner knows getting a dog is a responsibility and a privilege. The owner has thought of what they want from this dog, in other words what is the dogs job going to be? Is it to be a house companion, property deterrent, animal therapy dog, a companion for children, outdoor adventurer, gun dog, hunting dog, caring assistant dog? As you can see the list is endless and there are breeds out there that suit each of those roles. Additionally, there are great resources in the UK to meet these breeds in person, such as breeder's clubs and dog show events like Discover Dogs and Crufts.

So, get out there send some emails, do some research, and find the perfect dog breed for you.

Avoiding conflict

Dogs have learnt detailed communication due to being social creatures. Like us we need physical signs to illustrate our thoughts across to others, which in dogs can be used to de-escalate conflict within a social situation. Dogs are no different to us, we both need visible social cues to communicate. However, this manual is not going to go through each individual visible cue, mainly because they are too complex to explain only through words on a page. To be explained professionally, pictures and videos would be required. For example, it would be irresponsible to suggest a particular tail position means a particle sign. In a nutshell, this book would be simplifying what is going on and could result in the owner misunderstanding the situation. That is why this manual suggests taking a video of your dog's behaviour and sending them to a dog behaviourist or dog trainer if you are wanting to understand the dog's communication and motives.

Even though this manual will not go into detail about visible social cues, there are some topics that can be covered safely. A safe case that can be covered is when a dog shows its belly to another dog when being greeted. This is a defensive posture aimed at another dog, showing their submission. Some dogs will go straight into this position, which can be observed by a dog trainer as the dog being uncomfortable in that particular social situation, especially when it is combined with lip smacking. More than likely, they are communicating to the other dog that they are not a threat and would rather engage in a playful or positive manner.

The problems that occur with dog-to-dog communication is often not the dog's fault but the humans. In most cases of dogs having undesirable interactions with another dog, it can be resolved by the dogs being left alone. Allowing them to sort out the situation with each other, without human interference, dramatically reduces the chance of a dog becoming injured. For example, an owner sees an out-of-control puppy getting attacked by adults. That is not what is happening. The puppy is getting too excitable, reaching a point where they are going to be uncontrollable and in a pack situation that will lead to confrontation within the group of dogs. So, the older dog would often tell the puppy off. The young dog should go to the ground and show submission to its elders. By getting this response from the older dog, the puppy is shown what is tolerated in the dog's world, and how to act around older dogs.

It is common to see cases of owners protecting and encouraging this puppy madness, but eventually the puppy becomes a young adult with no polite social skills to communicate with other dogs. Being polite and knowing the social rules and steps are fundamental in the dog social world. Therefore, dogs that have been brought up with no social skills will often offend other dogs with their unpolite behaviour, which results in them being hurt on more than one occasion by other dogs.

"My training equipment does not work"

Training tools/equipment are often used to support or eradicate undesirable behaviours in a dog. The purpose of these tools is to the make the owners life easier and in some cases to reduce the training that is required. To be truthful no training tool works without the correct method on how to use it. Therefore, it is important to consult a local dog trainer if you feel that a piece of training equipment would be beneficial to you. Trainers are experienced in helping members of the public train their dogs to behave in the ways they desire. They understand how to use training equipment correctly and safely and are the fundamental tool in training. Without understanding how and why to use a particular training tool, it is a recipe for disaster.

Take a choke lead for example. This equipment is commonly used wrong, and it is frustrating to see this tool being used when it often causes more issues. It is designed to help the owner gain control of the dog's pulling. In the wrong hands it is becoming a common lead used in day-to-day walking. This only teaches the dog to get used to the tight feeling around its neck, which results in the dog pulling anyway.

Another example of a helpful tool is the clicker. A great way for the dog to understand that it has performed a desirable behaviour. It needs perfect timing and precision to be effective. Using a clicker during the training process in the manual would make life easier for you and the dog. However, it can be used in the wrong manner which can send mixed messages from the owner to the dog resulting in confusion and causing it to be harder for the dog to understand our true goal. That is why a professional prospective and demonstration would really be helpful to you and your dog.

We can use these tools to promote and enhance our objectives, such as misdirection. Misdirection can be used as an effective training method if done correctly. The idea is to use a piece of equipment like a specialised lead to redirect the mindset of a dog at a given time. This is a key technique when dealing with high energy behaviour demonstrations like fear-aggression or possessive actions.

In a nutshell, unless a dog trainer has shown you how to use a tool properly, it is not worth using them. It can cause more problems for you in the long run. Remember **IF IT IS NOT DIFFICULT IT IS NOT WORTH DOING.** Might be dramatic but it's true.

"I am going to be a dog trainer"

If you are reading this section, you must be having some thoughts of having a career as a dog trainer or behaviourist. You could already be an established trainer who is always keen to learn. Either way this section might interest you.

Firstly, I would like to say welcome to the club. It is not an easy career; it will require you to be adaptive and passionate in everything you do. Remember **there is always something new to learn**, so go out there and discover. To be successful in the career you need to be able to listen to all and be confident in trying out new methods and ideas.

The most important thing to be aware of when it comes to dog training and the public is that their overall idea on dog's roles and care methods will be constantly changing. Which is important as this will be your client base and understanding trends and new legislation will mould your training methods and professional advice. This can be a good thing as it allows you to think outside the box.

For example, in the professional dog community it is known and expected that at some point dog day care will be used by every dog owner and will become the standard practice. You are probably thinking "How does this help me as a dog trainer?" Well, these dog day care establishments want clients that have well trained dogs that like to socialise with others. Which is where we, as dog trainers, come in. Also, these facilities are the perfect location to train socially rehabilitated dogs in a controlled area.

So go out there and talk to other companies to link up with dog day care centres, dog groomers, local vets, hydrotherapy companies, dog walkers and other dog trainers. This will put you ahead of the game and help you understand how they operate.

The 4 don'ts of dog training

- Don't give a client medical advice
- Don't discredit another dog trainer
- Don't leave a dog in a dangerous or harmful environment
- Don't encourage dog on dog violence

One of the sad truths about dog training is you're not training the dog; you are training the owner.

In fact, it should be called human training. A good trainer will hear what that owner has to say but listens to the dog. A good dog trainer also knows that the dog will never lie, they will openly let you know how they perceive that situation. When walking into a client's home, the dog automatically tells you everything that goes on in the house and they will react with unsure behaviour if anything changes. Another key point is that dogs do not randomly do anything for no reason, they are always an honest pure at heart animal. After a while working with dogs, you will realise these animals have nothing to hide. These skills can be learned through education and experience so please don't read this and feel overwhelmed. In fact, reading this should inspire you to read more books on this subject and compare notes on what this manual has to say compared to other books. This will allow you to make your own perception on what works and does not work.

The fact you are reading this manual, highlights that you are eager to learn and develop on what you already know. Learn and enjoy this process, most people would love a lifestyle of working with dogs and making owners lives better. This industry is hard and will require your full dedication but coming from experience it's worth doing if you love being around dogs.

The final most important thing is do not find yourself giving advice that could get yourself in trouble. Be careful what you tell people, remember you're a professional and are selling a quality service. Therefore, **giving out personal medical advice is a big no,** leave it to the veterinary industry.

They are the experts, and you are most likely not medically trained. Can you imagine how they must feel finding out a dog trainer has been giving out medical advice. One way to look at this would be if you found out another industry (not training or behaviour related) was giving out contradictory advice about your training methods.

It is also worth mentioning you could possibly find yourself in the middle of a legal issue if anything went wrong with the dog. It must be frustrating for vets if they find out you are giving uneducated knowledge to their clients which results in them having to convince the client they are an expert in their own field. Their qualification ensures that they are the best source of knowledge when it comes to health requirements.

In conclusion, you have taken the time to read through this manual for dog training and are willing to learn, therefore you are heading in the right direction. Dogs are always willing to learn and always enjoy spending time with you. So go out there and become a fantastic dog trainer, whether that be becoming a professional dog trainer or a great dog owner. By building upon your knowledge, you can some day pass on your methods to the next generation of dog trainers.

Printed in Dunstable, United Kingdom

67621517R00045